DRUGS AND EATING DISORDERS

Dieting to extremes may lead to eating disorders.

DRUGS AND EATING DISORDERS

Clifford J. Sherry, Ph.D.

THE ROSEN PUBLISHING GROUP, INC.

NEW YORK

The people pictured in this book are only models. They in no way practice or endorse the activities illustrated. Captions serve only to explain the subjects of photographs and do not in any way imply a connection between the real-life models and the staged situations.

Published in 1994, 1999 by The Rosen Publishing Group, Inc.
29 East 21st Street, New York, NY 10010

Copyright © 1994, 1999 by The Rosen Publishing Group, Inc.

Revised Edition 1999

Library of Congress Cataloging-in-Publication Data
Sherry, Clifford J.
      Drugs and eating disorders/Clifford J. Sherry.
        p. cm.—(The Drug abuse prevention library)
      Includes bibliographical references and index.
          ISBN 0-8239-3005-x
          1. Eating disorders in adolescence—Juvenile literature. 2. Medication abuse—Juvenile literature.
          3. Appetite depressants—Juvenile literature.
          [1. Eating Disorders. 2. Drug abuse] I. Title.
          II Series.
          RJ506.E18S53 1994
          616.85'26—dc20   93-35719
                                    CIP
                                    AC

Manufactured in the United States of America

Contents

Introduction

Angie is fourteen. Her older sister, Simone, is a dancer. Their parents have always said that Simone was the athletic and attractive one while Angie was the smart one. Angie decided that she was tired of being just the smart one. She wanted to be the pretty daughter, the one the guys always called. She decided that she would be more attractive if she lost some weight.

A friend told her about some weight loss pills she could buy at the drugstore. Angie started taking the pills, and she also cut down on the amount of food she ate. She began skipping breakfast and having only an apple and a diet soda for lunch. At dinner she barely touched her food. Within a few months, Angie looked skeletal. Her parents,

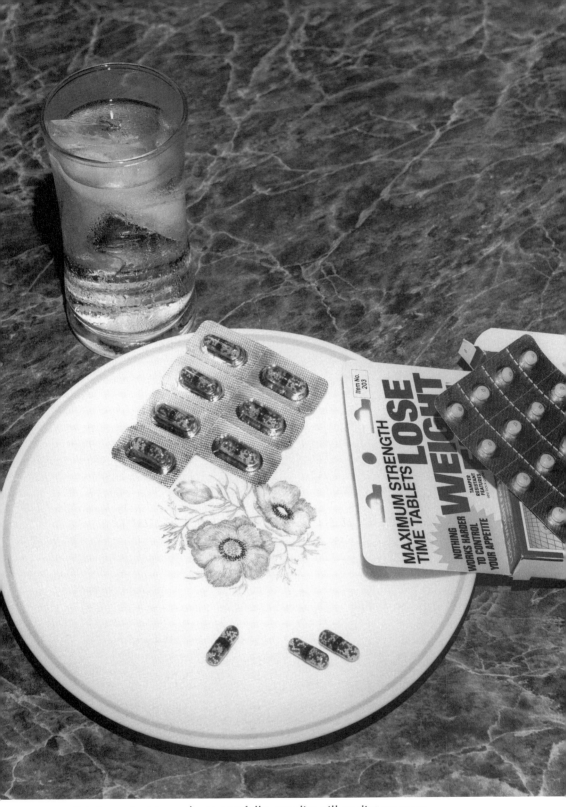

It is important to evaluate carefully any diet pill or diet program.

8 *sister, and friends were all worried about her, but Angie wanted to lose ten more pounds. She felt that way until the day she fainted and had to be rushed to the hospital. The doctors told her that if she had continued her eating habits, she could have died.*

There are many teens who feel the same way as Angie. Many young women and men have unhealthy eating habits and attitudes toward food. They are easily influenced by all forms of media—especially television, magazines, and movies—which send the message that skinny is sexy. These teens believe that to be attractive or successful they need to be thin. In their efforts to become skinnier, they may turn to drastic measures, such as diet drugs, to lose weight.

As a result, the sale of weight loss drugs has become a multimillion-dollar business. Each year more than $30 billion is spent on weight loss products.

FDA Approved Drugs

In the United States, the Federal Drug Administration (FDA) is the government agency that determines which drugs are safe to release to the public. Currently the only two over-the-counter drugs approved by the FDA for weight loss are benzocaine

and phenylpropanolamine (PPA). Although
the government considers these drugs to
be safe, they can have harmful effects.

Benzocaine is a local anesthetic. It
deadens the taste buds in the mouth, so
food will taste bland and you will want to
eat less often. Benzocaine is usually added
as an ingredient in diet candies or gum.

Phenylpropanolamine can be found in
diet products such as Dexatrim and
Acutrim. This drug is a stimulant that
increases brain and body activity. It causes
a temporary decrease in appetite and
allows food to remain in the stomach
longer, so you feel full.

Users may believe that PPA is safe
because it can be bought in any drugstore
without a prescription, but it can have
serious side effects. The FDA recommends
that people should not take PPA for more
than four to six weeks, and that they should
not take more than 75 to 150 milligrams
per day. Increased dosage can cause high
blood pressure, anxiety, and nervousness.
Long-term use or larger doses can lead to
depression, fatigue, and addiction.

There is another category of FDA-
approved drugs which have *not* been
shown to be effective weight loss products
but are used by many people as diet aids.

10 These drugs, which are sold as laxatives, form a bulky mass inside the stomach. Once swallowed, these agents absorb water and other liquids. If you take one of these drugs just before a meal, you may feel full and eat less. But these kinds of drugs can be dangerous. If not taken according to the directions, they pose serious health risks and can be addictive.

The most recent diet drug approved by the FDA is sibutramine, sometimes sold under the trade name Meridia. This drug works by suppressing the appetite. It is only to be used by people who are substantially overweight. Sibutramine can cause some side effects, such as increased blood pressure. Its use should be carefully monitored by a doctor. Meridia is to be used together with a reduced-calorie diet and an exercise program.

The FDA is very strict about testing a drug's safety before making it available to the public. But occasionally drugs that are released onto the market are found to have dangerous effects on some users. For example, in 1997 the FDA recalled two very popular weight loss drugs—dexfenfluramine (Redux) and fen-phen, a mixture of fenfluramine and phentermine. They found that 30 percent of Redux and fen-phen users had developed heart valve problems and that a number of users had died. Drugs, even those approved by the government, should always be used with caution and, if possible, with the advice of a doctor.

Diet Drugs and Eating Disorders
Like Angie, many people who use diet drugs try to speed up the weight loss process even further by cutting back on how much they eat. This begins an unhealthy relationship with food and can eventually lead to an eating disorder.

Recent studies show that eight million people in the United States suffer from an eating disorder. Without treatment, 20 percent of people who suffer seriously from eating disorders will die. But help is available. With treatment, only 2 to 3 percent will die. The recovery rate for those who get help is 60 percent.

This book will discuss the dangers associated with weight loss drugs as well as specific eating disorders and their risks. Many people with eating disorders are in denial about their problem. The first step is to get them to recognize that they have a problem; then they must seek help. With counseling and professional assistance, people with eating disorders can recover and live long and healthy lives.

Some teens have unrealistic expectations about their ideal body weight.

CHAPTER 1

How Does It All Begin?

Kathy is 18 years old and a senior in high school. She is a co-captain of the cheerleading squad. She is also a swimmer and gymnast. She is 5 feet 3 inches tall and weighs 120 pounds. Kathy is a well-proportioned and attractive young woman. But she thinks she is fat. She is not alone.

Everyone seems to want to be thin. Television, magazines, and the movies promote thinness. Love, happiness, and admiration are supposed to come with a slender figure.

Girls and young women have gotten the messages. The results of a survey of young girls were reported in the medical journal *Pediatrics*. They found that elementary school children thought it was worse to be

14 fat than to be handicapped or disabled. Even high school girls who were under-weight worried about getting fat.

Kathy started out the way many teen-age dieters do. She planned to eat nothing but a piece of dry toast a day. But she was hungry all the time, so she ate more than the dry toast. When she did eat other things, she felt bad. She felt like a failure. And she felt fat.

Diet Pills

She saw advertisements for diet pills on television. She read about them in maga-zines. The ads promised that the pills would help her control her appetite. They said the pills would help her lose weight. They said the pills would help her be thin.

Kathy started taking over-the-counter diet pills that contained PPA. She read the instructions on the package. She took only two pills each day. At first, she did feel less hungry. But within two weeks the two pills did not control her appetite. She was still hungry all the time. Soon Kathy was using as many as 10 boxes of pills per week. Even that amount was not enough to help her be the thin person she wanted to be. Kathy still felt fat. And she was still hungry all the time.

Water Pills

The pharmacy where Kathy bought her diet pills was fairly typical. It displayed diuretics (water pills) right next to the diet pills. Diuretics cause the kidneys to remove "excess" water.

Some women retain excess water in their tissues. This usually happens just before the menstrual period. It makes them feel uncomfortable. Removing the excess fluid relieves the discomfort.

The FDA approved water pills for this purpose. But it does not approve them as dieting aids. Why? Diuretics change many body functions. That is why most water pills are prescription drugs. They should only be used under a doctor's care.

Kathy did not know that the FDA does not approve the use of water pills as a diet aid. What she did know was that water pills were available.

She remembered that in biology class, the teacher said that 75 percent of the human body is water. Kathy weighs 120 pounds. So her body contains about 90 pounds of water. If she could lose just a little of that water, she would lose weight. She would be thin!

So Kathy bought some water pills. The pills she bought contained a chemical

16 called ammonium chloride. It takes from several hours to several days for these pills to begin to work. The normal dose is three grams a day. The tablets usually contain 0.5 gram of ammonium chloride. They are coated to protect the stomach. Kathy took six tablets a day.

Like pills containing PPA, more is not better. Higher doses of water pills cause stomach ache, nausea, and sometimes vomiting. Ammonium chloride works for only a few days.

Kathy could just as easily have bought pills containing pamabrom. Pamabrom usually doubles the output of urine for about an hour. No more than 200 milligrams should be taken in one day.

Pills from Plants

Water pills may also contain materials from plants. These include the dried leaves of bearberries, parsley, or ground juniper berries. These plant materials "work" by causing irritation of the kidney and urinary passages. However, one of the side effects of juniper berries is an increase in appetite.

Water pills usually contain more than one of the ingredients listed above and a painkiller, such as aspirin.

Dieting with pills can bring on various health problems.

18   Water pills also sometimes contain an antihistamine called pyrilamine. It tends to make you sleepy. Pyrilamine has other side effects: loss of appetite, nausea, vomiting, stomach ache, constipation, or diarrhea.

If Kathy lost one percent of her body water, she would be thirsty. At five percent she would be very thirsty. She probably could not keep from drinking. If she weighed 120 pounds, a five percent loss of body water would represent about six pounds of weight loss.

When Kathy urinates, she loses water, but she also loses potassium. Potassium is needed for normal functioning of the heart and the nervous system. If she loses too much potassium, she can have an irregular heartbeat. She can also have cramps. She could even die of heart failure.

Kathy unfortunately did not know that ammonium chloride only works for a few days. She continued to take the water pills, as well as pills containing PPA. She ignored pleas from her boyfriend and her parents. She would not stop her diet plan.

Kathy died in her sleep of heart failure, just before her 20th birthday. A few days before her death, she told her parents she was still too fat. She weighed 90 pounds!

CHAPTER 2

Other Diet Drugs

Ginny and her best friend Gwen started taking ballet lessons in eighth grade. They noticed that their teacher was really thin. And all the ballerinas they saw in pictures were really thin. Ginny and Gwen decided that they wanted to be really thin, too. So they made a pact. They would eat only carrots and celery for lunch.

They did this for several weeks and did not get really thin. So they made a new pact. They would not eat lunch at all. Ginny also stopped eating breakfast and ate only carrot sticks for dinner.

Ginny's parents did not pay much attention to her. They did not notice that she was not eating.

20

When Gwen stopped eating, her parents were worried. So they took Gwen to see Dr. Kyle, their family doctor. Dr. Kyle examined Gwen. He found that she was 5 feet 2 inches tall and weighed 93 pounds. Dr. Kyle showed Gwen and her parents a table in one of his medical books. Her height was about average for a girl her age, but she was a bit underweight.

Dr. Kyle gave Gwen a poster from the National Academy of Science. It showed pictures of the foods in the major food groups. It also explained that everyone needs vitamins and minerals, especially growing teenagers. A diet of 1,000 calories or less probably could not supply all of those needs.

Dr. Kyle told Gwen that she did not need to diet. He did say that she should continue ballet. It is an excellent form of exercise.

Gwen and Ginny were almost exactly the same size, except that Ginny weighed only 90 pounds. Gwen was excited and told Ginny what Dr. Kyle said.

But Ginny would not listen to Gwen. She continued dieting. She was hungry all the time. She saw an advertisement in a magazine for diet pills. She decided to try them.

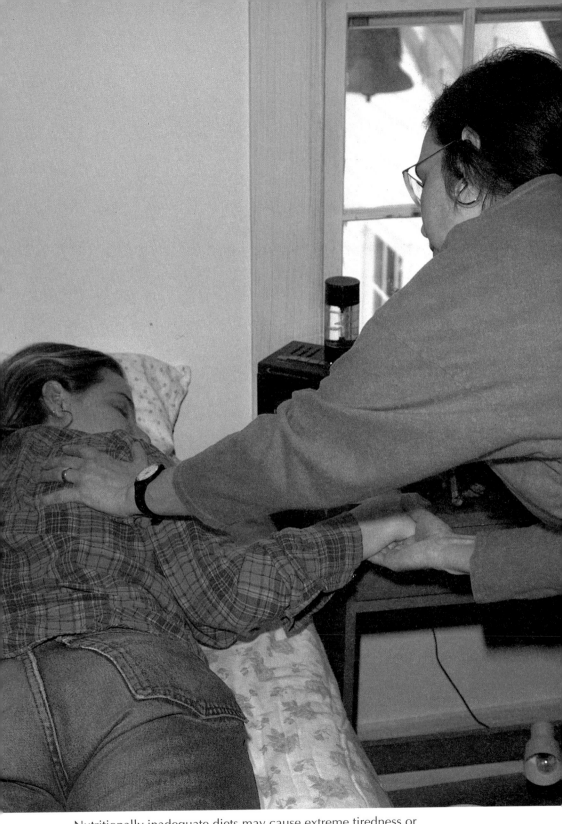

Nutritionally inadequate diets may cause extreme tiredness or serious illness.

22

Ginny bought a package of diet pills containing PPA. She followed the instructions on the package. She took only two pills a day just before meals. But the pills made her jittery.

Ginny had read an article in one of the tabloid newspapers at the supermarket checkout counter. It said that a movie star lost fifteen pounds without dieting. She had done it by eating a quarter-cup of whole bran cereal before each meal. The movie star said that because the bran formed a gel in her stomach, she didn't feel so hungry and thus ate less.

Ginny tried this for several days, but she didn't like the bran very much. So she stopped.

Laxatives
Then she saw an ad for a bulk-forming laxative pill. It contained carrageenan. Ginny had seen this chemical listed as an ingredient in ice cream, salad dressing, and other food products, so she thought it was safe. She bought some of the pills and tried them. They did seem to curb her appetite somewhat, but she didn't lose any weight or get thin.

Ginny noticed that there were many other kinds of laxatives at the pharmacy.

A diet of only carrots and celery is not enough to maintain good health.

24 Many of them were in the form of chocolate candy or chewing gum. Most of them
contained phenolphthalein. That chemical
works directly on the colon. It prevents
water and salt from being absorbed back
into the body. In six to eight hours it
causes a bowel movement that is watery.

Ginny bought a package and read the
instructions. After using it, she really got
scared when she noticed that her urine
was pink. She thought she was bleeding.
Her skin also broke out in burning itchy
patches. These are common side effects of
this kind of laxative. So she had to stop
taking it.

Ginny decided to try another brand.
She found one that contained a chemical
called bisacodyl. It works by stimulating
nerves in the colon. This type of laxative
can be harsh. It can cause mild cramps,
burning of the rectum, and abdominal
discomfort. It can also cause muscle weak-
ness and trembling.

Laxatives can also contain a variety of
plant products. Some of them are cascara,
senna, and aloe. They take six to eight
hours to work and cause a soft to semi-
liquid bowel movement. They can also
cause cramps or abdominal discomfort.
The urine may change color.

Ginny failed to realize one important point. Almost all of the nutrients in food are absorbed before the food reaches the colon. If too much is absorbed, you gain weight. If too little is absorbed, you lose weight. And if just the right amount is absorbed, your weight does not change.

Very few nutrients are absorbed in the colon. The colon absorbs some vitamins and minerals, but these do not cause a change in weight. So what happens in the colon actually has little effect on weight gain or loss.

Some experts call laxative use "the other form of drug abuse." This is because the colon can get used to the effects of the laxatives. Then the colon has difficulty causing a bowel movement without the laxative.

Ginny's Luck

Because she was away, Gwen did not see Ginny during the summer vacation. But when Gwen picked up her new school schedule, she learned that Ginny was in her first class, P.E. Gwen was shocked when she saw her friend. Ginny was so thin that her hip bones stuck out.

Gwen told her mom about Ginny that day after school. Gwen's mom called one

A friend or counselor may help you find the proper care for treating an eating disorder.

of the school counselors. The counselor talked to Ginny alone and then called her parents. He told Ginny's parents that their daughter needed help. She needed counseling. If she did not stop her dieting, she could become so thin that her body could not function normally. She could die.

Fortunately, Ginny was one of the lucky ones. She did get counseling. She was able to stop taking pills. And with Gwen's help, she was able to start eating.

A Sweet Tooth

Bart really liked sweets: chocolates, spice drops, cookies, cupcakes, ice cream, cheese cake, or anything sweet. He would eat until he could not eat any more. Really stuff himself!

It all started when he got to high school. In junior high, Bart had the highest grade point average in his class. He had never gotten less than an A in any subject. But in high school things changed. No one seemed to notice him. Then it happened! He took a chemistry exam and got a 62. His first D! And he was not doing very well in his other classes. Bart felt really bad. He ate a quart of Dutch chocolate ice cream, and he felt better. So he ate another quart of ice cream, then another.

Some people eat large amounts of sweets to make themselves feel good.

After a while Bart began to feel very sick. Eventually he vomited. Vomiting was unpleasant, but he found that after throwing up he could eat more. And eating more made him feel good.

The next day Bart stuffed himself again with doughnuts and cookies. As soon as he began to feel sick, he made himself vomit. Then he ate more. Soon Bart was making himself throw up every day. His grades were not improving, and he felt like he had no control over his schoolwork or his friends. No one seemed to understand him. The only thing that made him feel better was eating.

Bart also began to steal sweets to satisfy his binges. After several months he was able to make himself vomit simply by relaxing the muscles of his esophagus (the tube that leads from the mouth to the stomach).

Bart is now a grown man. His teeth and gums have become permanently discolored and damaged by the stomach acids that pass through his mouth each time he vomits. Bart's diet is lacking in many essential vitamins and minerals, so he catches colds easily and often feels weak and exhausted.

Bart is not happy with his lifestyle. He knows that he is hurting himself, and he

Many communities and schools are setting up programs to educate people about the dangers of drugs.

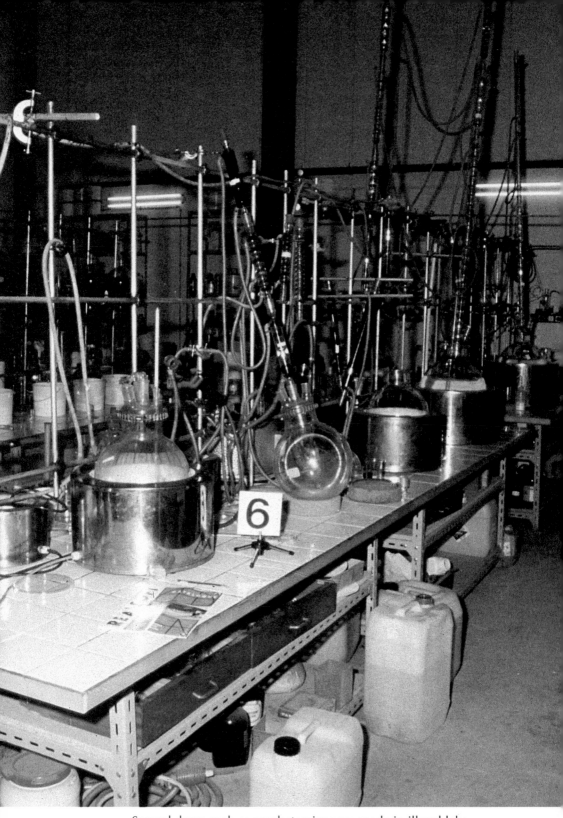

Several drugs such as amphetamines are made in illegal labs.

is aware that his behavior may eventually
pose deadly risks. But he does not know
how to change.

Amphetamines as Diet Drugs

There are three main categories of
amphetamines: methamphetamine,
dextroamphetamine, and levoamphetamine. These drugs are legal when prescribed by a doctor and purchased in a
pharmacy. However, they can also be
bought illegally on the street.

Amphetamines are stimulants. They
speed up both the body and brain, which
explains one of their most common street
names: "speed." Amphetamines seem to
give you extra energy. They also cause
euphoria, which means that they make you
feel happy.

Another effect of amphetamines is to
decrease appetite, so they are used in
many prescription diet drugs like
Methedrine, Dexoval, Dexedrine, and Ben-
zedrine. But some people turn to illegal
amphetamines bought on the street as
diet aids. Amphetamines—both legal and
illegal—can be very dangerous if misused.
Psychological effects include intense
anger and suicidal tendencies. Physical
dangers include fever, high blood pressure,

34 | vomiting, blackouts, and coma. In addition, because amphetamines speed up the heart rate and blood pressure, exercising while using them can cause a heart attack.

History of Amphetamines

Amphetamines were discovered about a century ago, but no one found a use for them until almost fifty years later. During World War II, soldiers were given amphetamines to increase their energy level and alertness. By the 1960s, doctors were regularly prescribing amphetamines to treat low blood pressure, depression, and other medical conditions.

Soon hospitals and doctors began reporting many serious problems. Young users of amphetamines were suffering from strokes and heart attacks, which are very unusual for people this age. Also, teenagers were becoming addicted to these stimulants. In response to these findings, doctors began to limit the amount of amphetamines they prescribed, and police cracked down on stores that sold the drugs illegally.

Illegal labs soon began appearing on the West Coast. The drugs produced in these labs were often contaminated or incorrectly manufactured. The labs could not hire trained chemists and frequently replaced unavailable chemicals with other substances. These labs spread to other regions of the country. They began producing various kinds of amphetamine-like stimulants.

Today the form of amphetamine most widely available on the street is a mixture of dextroamphetamine and levoamphetamine. The exact mixture depends on the skill of the person making the drug. It is usually diluted, or cut, with sugar or chalk.

Methamphetamine can also be bought on the street. It is known by many different names, including "speed," "crank," "chicken powder," "go-fast," "shabu-shabu," "go," "zip," "batu," "chris," and "christy." Pure methamphetamine hydrochloride, which is the strongest form of methamphetamine and looks like rock candy, is called "ice," "crystal," "glass," "quartz," or "L.A." According to a 1998 survey, 5.3 percent of high school seniors had used pure methamphetamine hydrochloride—up from 3.1 percent in 1993. Also, 16.4 percent of seniors had used some kind of stimulant. Undoubtedly some of these teens had used these drugs as weight loss aids.

36 | Diet Drugs

Legal diet drugs include both prescription and over-the-counter (OTC) drugs. Most prescription diet drugs are altered forms of amphetamines. Common prescription diet aids include benzphetamine (Didrex); chlortermine (Voranil); diethylpropion (Tenuate, Tepanil); phendimetrazine tartrate (Bontril, Plegine); phentermine HCl (Adipex-P, Fastin); and phentermine resin (Ionamin).

For a long time, drug companies have been searching for a prescription drug that suppresses the appetite without causing the dangerous side effects associated with amphetamines and PPA. At first, Redux and fen-phen seemed to be the solution. However, in 1997 the FDA removed both Redux and fen-phen from the market because of the serious dangers these drugs posed.

Over-the-counter drugs containing PPA are very popular in the United States. In fact, Americans spend more than $220 million a year on these products. However, most experts agree that these diet drugs work only for a short time, if at all. Diet aids made with amphetamines are stronger than those made with phenylpropanolamine, but amphetamine-based products reduce the appetite only temporarily and have many more dangerous side effects.

Sibutramine (Meridia), the newest FDA-approved diet drug, was placed on the market in 1997. Sibutramine works by affecting parts of the brain that control appetite. Experts emphasize that Meridia should be used in combination with a reduced-calorie diet and regular exercise.

Meridia, like all diet drugs, is not a "quick-fix" solution. These drugs can be helpful for some people, but they must be used as just one part of an overall health improvement plan. When taken without the supervision of a doctor, diet drugs— whether bought by prescription, over-the-counter, or on the street—can be very dangerous. The organizations listed at the back of this book can give you more information about the risks of these drugs and how to begin a healthy weight loss program.

CHAPTER 3

Eating Disorders

*I*t is estimated that over eight million people in the United States suffer from eating disorders. More than 90 percent of these people are female, though the number of males with eating disorders is on the rise. According to a recent study, one in about 400 males between the ages of thirteen and thirty has an eating disorder.

The most common eating disorders are anorexia nervosa (anorexia), bulimia nervosa (bulimia), and binge-eating disorder (compulsive eating). Five percent of teenagers and adult women and one percent of men suffer from one of these three disorders. About 15 percent of young American women have signifi-

Many girls start dieting at a very early age while their bodies are
still developing.

40 cantly disordered attitudes or behavior toward food.

Tina is 5' 2" and weighs 115 pounds. Although her doctor told her that her weight is within the normal range for someone her age and height, Tina feels fat. When she sees all the slim models in the magazines and the skinny, popular girls in her school, she often thinks that no one will ever find her attractive.

Tina begins a healthy regimen of exercise and low-fat, well-balanced meals. After three weeks, she has lost several pounds. However, she isn't satisfied with the amount of weight she has lost and how long it has taken. She wants more dramatic results in a shorter period of time. Soon she stops eating breakfast, then lunch. Before long, Tina develops a serious eating disorder—anorexia.

Anorexia Nervosa

Anorexia is one of the most common eating disorders. People suffering from anorexia nervosa take dieting to the extreme, literally starving themselves. They eat very little or nothing at all. People who suffer from this disorder often weigh only 85 percent or less of the normal weight for their age and height.

People with anorexia are called anorexics. They often have a distorted image of their bodies and are terrified of becoming fat. No matter how much they actually weigh, they still *feel* that they are fat. Even those who are severely underweight think that they need to lose weight.

Anorexia usually starts during adolescence (between twelve and eighteen years of age), but it can begin at any age. Many but not all people with anorexia start dieting by using weight loss pills, diuretics, and laxatives. These people display no early warning signs, aside from weight loss. Eventually, though, they begin to suffer from the following physical symptoms:

- Dry, pale skin and brittle hair
- Depression, irritability, and withdrawal
- Frequent light-headedness, headaches, or fainting spells
- Loss of menstruation in women and a drop in sexual hormones for men
- A growth all over the body of soft, downy hair called lanugo
- Damage to heart and kidneys, and possibly death

Bulimia Nervosa

Rosa is seventeen. She is exhausted. She has just spent the last five hours and four

Anorexics do not want to eat for fear of becoming overweight.

months' paychecks in three different restaurants. In each restaurant she ordered a full meal, including appetizer and dessert. And she ate every bit. Then she found a private place and vomited it all up.

Rosa has been vomiting so regularly that now all she has to do is tighten her stomach muscles. The food comes up with very little effort.

It all started about two years ago, when Rosa's boyfriend had graduated from high school and started college in a different state. For the first few months everything was fine, and nothing changed between them. They wrote to each other every day.

But one weekend Rosa's boyfriend came home to visit. When he told her that he was seeing another girl, Rosa felt hurt and betrayed. In junior high school she had been a "big fish" in a little pond: She had been a popular student, a member of the band, and a writer for her school newspaper. In high school Rosa felt like a "little fish" in a big pond. Now she didn't even have a boyfriend.

Rosa was crying when she told her older cousin Natalie about the breakup. Natalie suggested that they go to the food court at the mall and "pig out." So they did.

They ate everything in sight: ice cream sundaes, a bunch of chocolate eclairs, and

44 *anything else that was sweet and rich.*

By the time they got home, both girls felt sick. Natalie offered to tell Rosa a secret: She had been pigging out for years without gaining weight. She just made herself throw up.

So Rosa and Natalie made themselves vomit. Soon the pattern of overeating and vomiting became a habit. Rosa and Natalie would spend every weekend eating and then making themselves throw up.

After graduating from high school, Rosa went to college in another city and lost touch with Natalie. But she could not stop the cycle of bingeing and purging that she had begun in high school.

Rosa and Natalie suffer from bulimia. Bulimia, which is also known as bingeing and purging, is about twice as common as anorexia. It generally starts during late adolescence, but people of any age can become bulimic. The disorder usually begins after a stressful event, such as the breakup of a relationship.

People who suffer from bulimia, called bulimics, eat large amounts of food—especially fattening foods such as junk food and desserts—in very short periods of time. This is called bingeing. They then

get rid of the food, or purge themselves, **45**
hoping that their bodies will not have
time to absorb the calories. Vomiting is
the most common form of purging; some
people with bulimia also try to rid their
bodies of food by using laxatives. But
because the calories are absorbed before
the food reaches the large intestine, laxatives do not usually prevent weight gain.

Some people who suffer from bulimia
develop a related disorder called exercise
addiction. The disorder is also known as
exercise bulimia because sufferers try to
"purge" calories from their system by
exercising compulsively.

Unlike people with anorexia, who are
usually very thin, people with bulimia can
maintain a normal weight. Between binges
some people with bulimia go through
periods of extreme dieting. They will drastically cut the amount of food they eat
until they cannot diet any longer. Then
they begin to eat uncontrollably. After-
ward they feel guilty about bingeing and
purge themselves of what they have eaten.

People who suffer from bulimia often
have low self-esteem and believe they
would be better people if they were
thinner. Although they may appear cheer-
ful or happy on the outside, inside they

46 are depressed, lonely, and ashamed. Unlike people with anorexia, who are in denial about their disorder, people with bulimia often admit that they are hurting themselves. But these people cannot change their behavior. Bulimia is as dangerous as anorexia, and it can be deadly. The following are some physical effects of bulimia:

- Damaged gums and tooth enamel caused by stomach acid entering the mouth from frequent vomiting
- Fatigue, skin problems, and poor eyesight
- Potentially fatal tearing and bleeding of the esophagus caused by repeated vomiting
- Irregular menstrual cycle or even the loss of it
- Loss of important vitamins and minerals necessary for a healthy diet
- Damaged heart, kidneys, and bones

Binge-Eating Disorder
Binge-eating disorder, also known as compulsive eating, is similar to bulimia in that compulsive eaters binge frequently, consuming far more calories than their bodies can use. Unlike people suffering

Bulimics go through a cycle of bingeing and purging.

Strenuous exercise is another way bulimics try to control their weight.

from bulimia, however, binge eaters do not purge themselves of the food they eat.

Some compulsive eaters are able to remain thin by exercising or fasting, but most are overweight or obese. In general, compulsive eaters have very low self-esteem. They drastically diet to lose weight but then lose control and binge. In addition to bingeing, other typical behaviors of compulsive eaters are sneaking snacks throughout the day and grazing, or overeating at different times and places during the day.

It is believed that binge eaters, like people with bulimia, use food as a source of comfort or to numb painful feelings. Binge eaters learn to eat in response to emotional rather than physical needs. As a result, they can't distinguish between real physical hunger and psychological "hunger." Because of this, compulsive eaters continue to feel hungry even after eating more than enough.

Eating disorders can be deadly if not treated properly. The good news is that help is available, and it does work. If you think you may have an eating disorder, the first step is to admit that you have a problem. Only then will you be able to find help and begin the path to recovery.

Often people with eating disorders will simply pick at or rearrange their food and pretend that they are eating.

CHAPTER 4

Where Can You Find Help?

Maryanne's parents were concerned about her. At 16, she was 5 feet 3 inches tall. That is about average for her age. An average girl her age should weigh about 117 pounds. But Maryanne weighed only 90 pounds. Almost all her friends weighed more than she did. Maryanne thought she was too fat. She talked about her weight all the time. She did not seem to think about anything else. And she did not eat.

Maryanne's problems started when she was 14. Her parents first noticed it at dinner time. Maryanne would come to the table and play with her food, but not eat it. She did not gain weight. She was tired all the time. Her periods stopped.

52 Maryanne's parents took her to visit the family doctor. Dr. Connors talked to Maryanne. He took a blood sample. He weighed Maryanne and measured her.

Dr. Connors said that Maryanne was suffering from anorexia nervosa. She was tired because she was not eating enough. She did not have enough red blood cells.

Dr. Connors said that Dr. Jones, a specialist in internal medicine, should examine Maryanne. Dr. Jones would head a team of professionals to treat Maryanne. The team would also include a counselor, a gynecologist, and a nutritionist.

Dr. Jones would deal with physical problems. He would monitor Maryanne for kidney problems and watch her heart carefully. Low blood pressure and slow heart rate are common complications of anorexia. He would also help Maryanne deal with bloating and dry skin.

Maryanne had admitted that she often used laxatives. So Dr. Jones would help her deal with muscle and stomach cramps, indigestion, and nausea that resulted from laxative abuse. Dr. Jones would also help Maryanne decrease her dependence on laxatives.

When Maryanne and her parents visited Dr. Jones, he told them that Maryanne

Prolonged eating disorders may indicate the need for a doctor's help.

54 needed counseling. Counselors can work with individuals. They also work with groups of people who meet to discuss similar problems.

A variety of therapists and counselors are available. Psychiatrists are medical doctors. They specialize in treating people with mental problems. They can prescribe drugs as part of the treatment.

Psychologists and social workers also treat people with mental problems. They generally have specialized training in their fields, but they cannot prescribe drugs.

A license is required to practice therapy (treatment). The therapist must have a certain level of training and experience before he or she can obtain a license.

A license, however, does not guarantee that a counselor or therapist is competent or ethical. But it is a start. It is important to meet the person. Ask about his or her training and experience with eating disorders. Find out how much the sessions will cost. Dr. Jones strongly recommended that Maryanne see Dr. Michaels.

Dr. Michaels told Maryanne's parents that she could not determine how long the treatment would take until she had more information. Dr. Michaels explained that it depends on several factors. One factor

is how long the illness has been going on.
Another is how severe the illness is. If
Maryanne had problems with drugs or
alcohol, it would make therapy more
complicated.

It is also difficult to know how a patient
will react to therapy. Some become angry
and defensive. Others act as if a black
cloud has been lifted from their lives.

Dr. Michaels explained that she wanted
to see Maryanne each week. She planned
to ask Maryanne's parents to come to
some of the sessions. She said it was very
important to keep the lines of communica-
tion open. Family meetings are one way
to do this. The family members must not
attack one another. They must stop making one another feel guilty. If they listen to
one another's problems, they may be able
to understand what went wrong and how
to work things out.

Other Helping Groups

Self-help groups are designed only for the
person with the problem. They are made
up of people with the same kind of problem. They meet regularly to discuss their
experiences and explore their feelings.

Support groups are for the family and
friends of the person with a particular

56 problem, such as an eating disorder. They can give emotional support. They can provide information about eating disorders and treatments. They can also help to cope with problems associated with eating disorders.

These groups are usually not run by therapists. Many groups invite guest speakers. Some just get together to talk and share ideas. They are usually free.

Fact Sheet

- Each year people in the United States spend more than $30 billion on weight loss products.

- About 80 percent of ten-year-old girls claim to be on a diet. Seventy-seven percent of teenage girls want to lose weight.

- About 31 percent of women diet at least once a month.

- Although around forty-four million people actively diet each year, 90 to 95 percent do not keep off the weight. Some actually gain back more weight than they lost.

- Laxatives do not help to rid the body of calories already consumed. By the time the food reaches the

58 intestines, the body has already absorbed the calories.

• Nine out of every ten people with an eating disorder develop it by the age of twenty.

• Although eating disorders usually affect teenagers and young adults, children as young as six and adults as old as seventy-six can also suffer from them.

• Today seven million women and one million men suffer from either anorexia nervosa or bulimia.

• With treatment, about 60 percent of those with eating disorders will survive.

• Without treatment, 20 percent of people with serious eating disorders will die.

Glossary

amphetamine Stimulant that depresses appetite temporarily.

anorexia nervosa Eating disorder in which the person has an intense fear of becoming obese.

benzocaine Local anesthetic used in hard candy or chewing gum to deaden the taste buds and make food have less flavor.

binge The eating of large amounts of food in a relatively short time.

body image The mental picture a person has of his or her appearance.

bulimia Eating disorder in which the person overeats (binges) and then vomits (purges).

eating disorder An obsessive interest in food, eating, and body weight.

60 **over-the-counter** A drug or a medical device that can be purchased without a doctor's prescription.

phenolphthalein A compound found in some chocolate-flavored tablets or chewing gum laxatives.

phenylpropanolamine A close chemical relative of amphetamine. It causes a temporary decrease in appetite.

purge An attempt to get rid of excess food and calories following a binge. The most common form of purging is vomiting.

Where to Go for Help

In the United States:

**American Anorexia/
  Bulimia Association
  (AABA)**
165 West 46th Street
Suite 1108
New York, NY 10036
(212) 575-6200
Web site: http://www.
  members.aol.com/

**Anorexia Nervosa and
  Related Eating Disor-
  ders, Inc. (ANRED)**
P.O. Box 5102
Eugene, OR 97405
(541) 344-1144
Web site: http://www.anred.com

**Eating Disorders Aware-
  ness and Prevention, Inc.
  (EDAP)**
603 Stewart Street
Suite 803
Seattle, WA 98101
(206) 382-3587
Web site: http://members.
  aol.com/edapinc

**National Association of
  Anorexia and Associated
  Disorders (ANAD)**
P.O. Box 7
Highland Park, IL 60035
(847) 831-3438

Web site: http://www.
  members.aol.com/anad20

**National Eating Disorder
  Organization (NEDO)**
445 East Grandille Road
Worthington, OH 43085
(918) 481-4044
Web site: http://www.
  geocities.com/HotSprings/
  5704/edlist.htm

**Overeaters Anonymous
  (OA)**
P.O. Box 44020
Rio Rancho, NM 87174-4020
(505) 891-2664
Web site: http://www.
  overeatersanonymous.org

In Canada:

**Anorexia Nervosa and
  Associated Disorders
  (ANAD)**
109-2040 West 12th Street
Vancouver, BC V6J 2G2
(604) 739-2070

**The National Eating Dis-
  order Information Centre**
College Wing, 1st floor
Room 211
200 Elizabeth Street
Toronto, ON M5G 2C4
(416) 340-4156

For Further Reading

Barrett, CeCe. *The Dangers of Diet Drugs and Other Weight-Loss Products.* New York: Rosen Publishing Group, 1999.

Berry, Joy. *Good Answers to Tough Questions About Weight Problems and Eating Disorders.* Chicago: Children's Press, 1990.

Bode, Janet. *Food Fight: A Guide to Eating Disorders for Pre-Teens and Their Parents.* New York: Simon and Schuster, 1997.

Cooke, Kaz. *Real Gorgeous: The Truth About Body and Beauty.* New York: W. W. Norton, 1996.

Crook, Marion. *Looking Good: Teenagers and Eating Disorders.* Toronto: NC Press, Ltd., 1992.

Hall, Liza F. *Perk! The Story of a Teenager with Bulimia.* Carlsbad, CA: Gürze Books, 1997.

Kolodny, Nancy J. *When Food's a Foe: How You Can Confront and Conquer Your Eating Disorder.* Boston, MA: Little, Brown and Company, 1992.

Kubersky, Rachel. *Everything You Need to Know About Eating Disorders: Anorexia and Bulimia.* Rev. ed. New York: The Rosen Publishing Group, 1998.

Pipher, Mary. *Hunger Pains.* New York: Ballantine Books, 1997.

Index

64

About the Author

Dr. Clifford J. Sherry is a senior scientist with Systems Research Laboratories. He has taught human physiology and psychopharmacology to more than 2,000 students. He has publications in more than twenty-five scientific journals. He also writes magazine articles that focus on making science, medicine, computers, and the law understandable to nonspecialists.

Photo Credits

Cover: Dick Smolinski.
Pages 30–31: © John Berry/Gamma-Liaison; p. 32: © Gamma-Liaison. All other photos by Stuart Rabinowitz.